1. Introduction

Suicide is commended as an escape from the ills of life, and riches are to be despised. Aelian's Stoicism hardly goes below the surface. His primary object is to entertain and while so doing to convey instruction in the most agreeable form.

He was among the first to break away from the age-long tradition of the periodic structure of sentences, at least for works of a serious nature, and to affect a simpler prose of short, coordinated, sometimes paratactic, clauses.

In this and in the rich variety of topics and in a certain fondness for piquant, not to say earthy, stories from the life of men and of animals one may trace the influence of the Milesian Tales.

Unfettered by any canons of style or language, picaresque, and sometimes gross, they pandered to popular taste. To adopt their technique while refining the style and imparting a moral flavour to his narratives may well have seemed to Aelian a sure way of gaining a like popularity with educated readers.

Some might find fault with his random and piece-meal handling of his theme-of that he is well aware, and in the Epilogue he defends himself with the plea that a frequent change of topic helps to maintain the reader's interest and saves him from boredom.

But as to the permanent value of his work he has no misgivings, and since. Philostratus informs us that his writings were much admired, we may assume that they appealed to cultivated circles in a way that the voluminous and possibly arid compilations of grammarians did not.

2. The Red Mullet

I have spoken above of the Red Mullet, but The Red what I did not mention then I will now. At Eleusis it is held in honour by the initiated, and of this honour two accounts are given. Some say, it is because it gives birth three times in a year; others, because it eats the Sea-hare, which is deadly to man. I shall perhaps recur to the Red Mullet.

Flying-fish
Squids, Flying Gurnards, "and Flying-fish when scared fly and leap out of the sea. Squids leap furthest with the aid of their fins and rise high and are borne along together in flocks like birds.
Flying- fish Wing their flight at a lower level. The Flying Gurnards however move at so little distance above the surface of the sea, that you can hardly tell that they are not swimming but flying.

Fish moving information
It seems that Fishes roam and wander about, some in masses, like troops of animals or bands of hoplites marching in ranks or in lines, others advance in an orderly column; others again you would say were in companies.

Animal Peculiarity Volume 3 Part 2

By T.P Just

~~~

Copyright © 2010 by Terence Just. All rights reserved.

Get All The Books In The Series:

Animal Peculiarity Volume1 Part [1-8]
Animal Peculiarity Volume2 Part [1-8]
Animal Peculiarity Volume 3 Part [1-8]
<u>Just Enterprises</u>

Table of Contents

Others are numbered off by tens and swim together in that formation; there are even some that swim in couples, while there are others that remain at home in their lairs and spend' their lives there.

3. Various treatments for domestic animals

I have ascertained that skilled herdsmen when wishing to fatten their animals remove their horns. And when they wish to stimulate their he-goats to couple, they rub perfume on their nostrils; they even anoint their chins as well.

On the other hand they restrain an excessive appetite by tying a cord round the middle of the animals' tails. And Aristotle asserts that mares miscarry if for some length of time they smell an extinguished lamp wick.

I have heard also of this device to stop house-dogs from running away: they measure the length of their tail with a rod, smear the rod with butter, and then give it to the dog to lick. And the dogs remain at home, they say, as though they were fastened up.

How to Silence Dogs and Donkeys

Here is another peculiarity of Dogs. They will not bark if one approaches them holding the tail of a marten; but after cutting off the said tail of the captured marten, one must let it go alive. And a. Donkey will not bray if you suspend a stone from its tail, so they say.

The Elephant

In the season of summer when the sun's blaze is at its strongest Elephants smear one another with thick slime: this affords them coolness and is more agreeable to the aforesaid animals than a home beneath a cave or embowered in trees and branches.

They are good at tracking by scent and have a very keen sense of smell. At any rate on the march one precedes another, and the leader (they move in single file) takes note of the grass at his feet, and when he realises from the brushing that men have passed that way, he pulls up the grass and gives it to the elephant behind him to smell, and he in turn to the one behind him.

And this exchange, as you might call it, goes through the whole herd, until it comes to the one who is bringing up the rear, when he trumpets loudly. Whereupon like soldiers at a signal they turn aside to vales and thickets in the mountains or to low-lying marshes or even to level country where the bushes are dense.

But at all costs they avoid land which is trodden by men, for man is a creature whom they suspect as their worst enemy. And when their feeding-grounds fail some of them dig up roots and eat them, while others go off in search of fodder. And the Elephant that is the first to find what he is seeking turns back and calls his fellows and leads them to his lucky discovery.

4. Fish in winter

In the severest winter when the sea is stormy and the winds are blowing fierce and strong, Fish dread their native and beloved sea. And some of them heap up sand with their fins and so covered keep themselves warm, while others slip beneath some rock and are glad to rest sheltered from the cold.

Others again hasten down to the recesses of the sea and there below in the depths avoid the agitation from above. For, men say, the furies of the waves does not at that depth swell and batter them as it does above.

But at the beginning of spring when the sky grows bright and plants begin to put forth their leaves and the fields to wave with their natural herbage, the Fish observing that the sea is smooth and calm, mount up and leap about and Swim close to the shore as though they were returning from a long Journey.

Longevity of the Elephant

These, it seems, are the three creatures which from the smallest beginnings grow to the largest size: among aquatic animals the Crocodile, among birds the Ostrich, and among quadrupeds the Elephant.

And Juba relates that his father possessed an Elephant of a great age that was descended from remote ancestors; and that Ptolemy Philadelphus had an Ethiopian Elephant which had lived for many years and partly from its association with men and partly from its training had become exceedingly docile and gentle.

He also tells of an Elephant from India which belonged to Seleucus Nicator, and he says moreover that. it survived down to the supremacy of the Antiochi.

5. Sea-fish spawns in fresh water

All Fish that have a river or some lake near to their native sea, when they are about to spawn swim out of the salt water, choosing in preference to the waves water that is calm and not at all up heaved and lashed by gales.

For the tranquility of river and lake is well adapted to receive their offspring and to preserve their young from harm and from attack, both for other reasons and especially because of the absence or paucity of savage creatures.

And lakes and rivers normally enjoy this freedom. That is the reason why the Euxine abounds in such a quantity of fish: it has not learnt to foster monsters. If it does breed the seal and dolphins, they are of the smallest, but from all other pests the fishes here are protected.

6. The Pipefish

Pipefish's are slender, and having no womb to contain their foetus they are unable to endure the growth of their young within their bodies, but burst open; and in this way they do not give birth to, but eject, their offspring.

7. The bite of the Asp

It is said that the traces and indications of the bites of the Asp are far from evident or easy to detect. And the reason for this is, I learn, as follows. The Asp's poison is exceedingly sharp and spreads very rapidly.

So when the Asp fastens on a man the poison does not remain on the surface but penetrates to the inner passages of the body and disappears from view and from the skin before one's eyes, and presses inwards.

That, you see, is why the manner of Cleopatra's death was by no means easily recognized by Octavian's companions, but only after a time when two punctures, hard to detect and discover, were observed, and through them was revealed the riddle of her death. Besides, marks of the Asp's trail were visible, and they were clear to persons acquainted with the movements of these creatures.

Death of a snake-charmer

When Pompeius Rufus was Aedile at the Panathenaea a medicine-man, one of those who keep snakes for show, amid a crowd of his fellow- practitioners applied an asp to his arm in order to demonstrate his skill, and was bitten.

Thereupon he sucked out the poison with his mouth. He failed however to swallow some water afterwards, there being none at hand although he had got some ready (the vessel had been upset by an act of treachery), and as he had not washed off the poison and thoroughly rinsed his mouth he passed away after, I believe, two days Without suffering any pain, though the poison had little by little reduced his gums and his mouth to putrescence.

8. Fishes and their mating

When spring is at its height and the earth is putting forth her blossoms, animals are filled with an amorous impulse and bethink them of wedlock, and all that dwell in mountain or sea or that fly in the air desire to embrace one another. Among the Fishes there are some that rub off their eggs, massed and clinging together, on the sand; others as they swim spawn a great quantity of eggs, most of which are swallowed by those that swim in the rear. In fact the males lead the way and scatter milt, and the females that follow, open-mouthed and quite in- satiable, swallow it.

This is their method of coupling. I have explained above how some fishes actually live with the females and look after them as though they were their wives and that even among the various kinds of fishes the fires of a sort of jealousy break forth.

Fresh water in the sea

Aristotle and Democritus before him and third in order Theophrastus assert that fish are not nourished by salt water but by the fresh water that is mingled with the sea. And since this seems almost incredible, the son of Nicomachus, wishing to confirm the statement by actual practice, says that in every sea there is some drinkable water, and that it can be proved in this way. If one makes a thin, hollow vessel of wax and lets it down empty into the sea, having attached it so that it can be hauled up, after a night and a day it is, when drawn up, full of fresh and drinkable water. And Empedocles of Agrigentum asserts that there is some fresh water in the sea, not indeed perceptible to all, though it does nourish fishes. And this sweetening of the water in the brine he says is due to natural causes, which you may learn from his writings. It is said that those who have been initiated into the Mysteries of the two goddesses will not touch Dog-fish, for (they say) it is no clean food, since it gives birth through its mouth.

Some however maintain that it does not do so, but that when its young have been frightened by attempts on their life, it swallows and hides them away and that when the scare has passed, it again ejects them alive.

And these same initiates would not taste of a Red Mullet, nor would the priestess of Hera at Argos. The reasons for this I know that I have explained above somewhere.

9. Mating of Viper and Moray

I have not forgotten that I have in a previous passage told of the mating of Viper and Moray and how they couple, the Moray emerging from the sea, the Viper from its den. But what I did not tell, I now will.

When the Viper intends to couple with the Moray, in order to appear gentle as befits a bridegroom, he disgorges and throws up his poison, and then with a soft hissing sound, as though raising a kind of pre-nuptial Wedding chant, summons his bride.

And when they have together completed their amorous revels, the fish makes for the waves and the sea, while the snake gulps down his poison again and goes back to his native haunts.

10. An Elephant's jealousy

The Elephant is seldom in love, they say, for, as I have remarked earlier on, it is sober. And yet I learn of Elephants experiencing the passion of love, and the tale is one to excite astonishment. And this is what I have learnt.

A man who had some knowledge of the method of hunting these animals obtained leave from the Roman Emperor and set out to hunt them in the manner of the natives of Mauretania.

He tells in his narrative how he saw a young female Elephant, comely as Elephants can be, coupling with a young and beautiful male, while another older male (whether it was the husband or the lover of the aforesaid female) was furious as though it had been scorned.

For inflamed with violent passion it rushed forward and coming up to the young and beautiful Elephant, fell upon it and began to fight, like a man filled with resentment over the conduct of his wife or his mistress.

And the two dashed together with such force that both damaged their tusks. And neither was victorious, but the hunters separated them by hurling missiles at them, for the animals were helpless as soon as they were deprived of their weapons.

11. The 'Areion' Snail

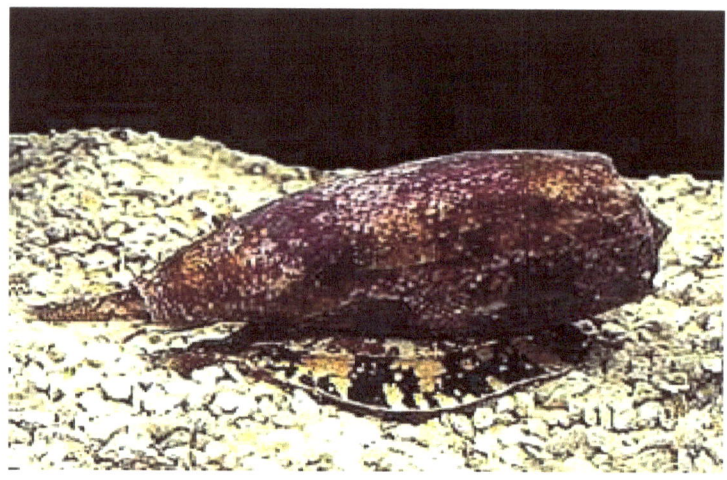

Snails know that partridges and herons are their enemies; so they escape from them, and in places where these birds feed you would never see snails crawling about. But the snails which they call Areiones deceive and elude the aforesaid enemies by natural astuteness.

Thus, they emerge from their native shells and feed without anxiety, while the birds which I mentioned swoop upon the empty shells as though they were the actual snails, but finding nothing, throw them aside as useless and go away. But the Areiones return and pass each to its own house, having eaten their fill of food and having preserved their lives by their deceptive migration.

12. The Spanish mackerel

It seems that the Spanish Mackerel of the Euxine imitate the Persian King who spends the winter at Susa and the summer in Ecbatana. For these fish pass the winter in the Propontis as it is called, since that region is warm, but in the summer they live about Aegialus, because the first-named sea affords them gentle breezes.

Cooking a Red Mullet

I am informed that when Cooks who are masters of their art wish the stomachs of Red Mullets not to burst in the cooking, they kiss their mouths. And if this is done the fish are preserved whole, so they say.

13. The Dolphin and its young

The female Dolphin has breasts like a woman and suckles its young with a liberal and copious supply of milk. And they swim in a body, but separated according to age. In the front rank are ranged the young and tender, after them swim the full-grown ones.

The Dolphin loves its offspring and is an affectionate creature, anxious for its children, and in order to protect them, as with soldiers in line of battle, some are with the front rank, others with the second, and others with the third.

The young ones swim in front, after them swim the females, and the males bring up the rear while they superintend and guard closely their offspring and their wives as they swim.

14. The Viper

Some maintain that the difference between the Echis and the Echidna is one of sex and not of kind, the former being the male viper, the latter the female. Others however consider that the difference is one of kind, and that the latter belongs to one species and the former to another.

And I hear some say that those who have been bitten by the Echis are seized with convulsions, whereas victims of the Echidna are not.

But others assert that the bite caused by the Echidna is white, unlike that of the Echis which is livid. And Nicander says that in the bite which the Echis implants traces of two fangs are visible, but more if it is an Echidna that has bitten.

15. Taming an Elephant

It is worth relating what men do after a successful Elephant-hunt to make the creatures docile and tame. First of all they lead them away bound into a wood a little distance from the trench in which they have captured them, keeping them apart by ropes and not allowing them either to run forward or to stop and pull back.

Next they fasten each beast to a very large tree at a measured distance from the next one so that they can neither spring forward nor retreat backwards to any extent through being free to leap about and work mischief.

And by refusing them food and by starvation they drain away their excessive strength and power, and gradually reduce their spirit and their inflexible determination, so that they forget their hitherto indomitable fierceness and abandon their former temper.

The keepers of these animals go up to them and offer them food from their hands, and the Elephants under stress of need take it and do the men no harm, and already begin to wear a mild and fatigued expression.

But those that are extremely powerful and full-grown, after bursting their bonds and tearing up trees with the points of their tusks and with their trunks, even smashing some by their onset and by assailing them, have with difficulty and only after a long While been tamed sometimes by starvation sometimes by pleasant food, at other times by means of goads. While these animals are being tamed their food consists of very large loaves of bread, barley, dried figs, raisins, onions, garlic, honey in large quantities, bundles of mastic branches and of palm-leaves and of ivy and any edible and familiar substance which is for that reason welcome to them

16. Vocal Fishes

Those who condemn all fishes without exception to silence are ignorant of their nature, because there are those that whistle and those that grunt. The Gurnard grunts, so too do the Chromis and the Caprus, as Aristotle says. The John Dory whistles; the Cuckoo (or 'Piper ') has a voice which resembles that of the bird whose name it bears and makes a similar sound.

The Flesh of the Elephant

To the eye the Elephant is a mass of flesh and of enormous size, but his flesh is not edible, excepting his trunk, the lips of his mouth, and the marrow of his tusks. But it seems that the fat of an Elephant is detested by poisonous creatures, for if a man rubs himself with it or burns some, they flee away to a great distance.

The Fauna of Arabia

The variety of colour and of shape in the fauna of Arabia might well put anyone skilled in painting to the test, not only in the case of powerful and noble animals but even of the more insignificant, the locusts and the snakes; for the markings on them look like gold.

The fish, which enjoy an even more richly wrought colouring, are an astonishing sight. And the oysters in the Red Sea are not without the same glamour, for they are encircled with rings of fiery hue, and to look at them you would say that with the blending of their colours they were copying the rainbow, Nature having painted parallel stripes upon them.

17. The Pearl

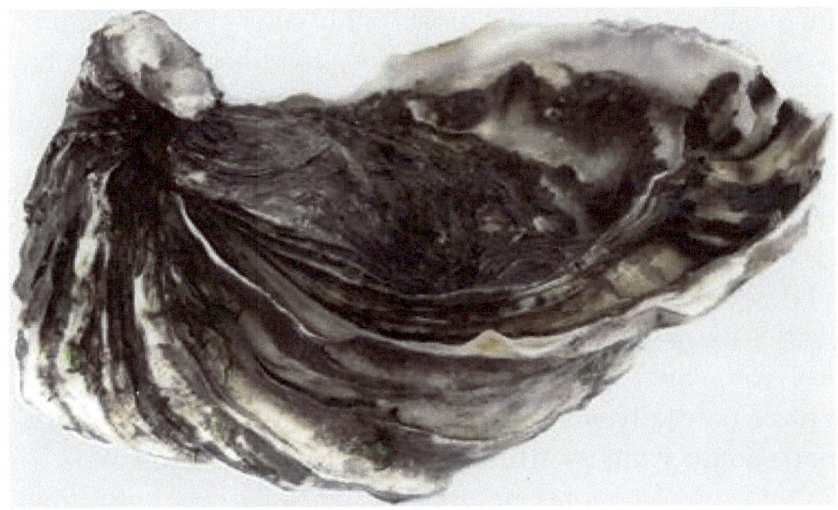

And the pearl, so celebrated among fools and admired by women, is also a nursling of the Red Sea, and they tell a marvelous story of how it is produced when flashes upon the open shells lightning.

So then these shells which are the mothers of the aforesaid pearls are sought for when the weather is fine and the sea smooth. And the seekers collect them and extract this object which delights the hearts of the luxurious.

One may find a small pearl even in the largest shell and a. large one in a small shell; and this one contains none, and that not more than one, and many contain a number. Some assert that as many as twenty have been attached to a single Shellfish.

Now the shell is the flesh, and these pearls cling to it like a thorn. But if one were to open the shell prematurely, that is before the birth-process is complete, one would find the flesh indeed, but it will not contain the object of one's quest.

The pearl, it seems, is like a stone produced by petrifaction, and it is not its nature to contain or to admit even a drop of moisture. In the opinion of those who trade in pearls and those who buy them pearls that are pure white and large are the most beautiful and the most highly esteemed, and I can avow that many of those who make a livelihood by them have become wealthy.

And I am also well aware that when these stones have been extracted and the Shellfish have been released after giving up the aforesaid coveted object as ransom for their lives, they have gradually produced another one.

If however the animal that fosters the pearl dies before the pearl is extracted, as is sometimes reported, both pearl and flesh rot away and perish.

It has a naturally smooth and well-rounded contour, but if a man should want by artificial means to make round and smooth some stone not naturally so, the pearl confounds his design, for it declines to yield and develops roughness's, thereby denouncing the plot that has been laid to secure its beauty.

18. The Hawk

The Egyptians appear to regard the Hawk as sacred to Apollo, calling the god 'Horus' in their own language, and they regard the birds with wonder and are right in saying that they belong to the aforesaid god.

For Hawks are the only birds that can face with ease and without pain the rays of the sun and are not the least dazzled; and while they fly at an immense height the divine fire does not trouble them at all.

Moreover observers say that the Hawk flies upside down, like a man swimming on his back, and in this way, you see, it looks at the sky and the all-surveying sun with complete freedom and without flinching.

It is the bitter enemy of snakes and venomous creatures. At any rate no snake, no scorpion, nor indeed any other product of noxious matter would escape its notice. Fruits and seeds it will not touch; it delights to feed on flesh and drinks blood, and on these it feeds its young; it is also passionate in lechery.

If the bone from its tibia is put beside gold it attracts and draws it to itself by some inexplicable fascination, persuading it to follow even as, they say, the stone of Heraclea somehow bewitches iron.

The Egyptians assert that the Hawk's life extends to as much as five hundred years, and they do not convince me: I merely report what have heard. Homer, they say, seems to hint that the Hawk is beloved of the child of Zeus and Leto (i.e. Apollo) when he says ' And down the hills of Ida he went, like unto a swift hawk, the slayer of doves.'

19. The Scarab

The Scarab is a creature of which there is no female, but it pours its semen into the heap which it rolls up. After doing this and keeping the heap warm for eight-and-twenty days, on the following day it brings forth its young.

Among the Egyptians the fighting class wore a Scarab engraved on their finger-rings, their ruler intimating thereby that those who fight for their country must at all costs and in every way be men, because the Scarab has in it nothing of the feminine element.

The Elephants love of home

Elephants when withdrawn from the country to which they are accustomed, though tamed at first by captivity and hunger and after that by food and a varied diet, nevertheless do not erase from their memory the spell of the country that fostered them.

At any rate the majority dies of grief, and some have actually lost their sight through the floods of tears past measuring which they have shed. And they are brought on board ships by means of a bridge on either side of which boughs fresh and in full leaf have been fixed, together with other greenery that extends the whole length in order to deceive the beasts.

For if the Elephants see these things they imagine that they are still walking on firm ground, and this verdure does not allow the sea to be visible. But the water close to the shore from which they must sail is shallow and not deep, and the cargo-vessels are some distance out. That is why there is need of the bridge and the device of a ruse contrived with the boughs and greenery aforesaid.

20. The Ram

I have heard that the Ram during the six months of winter lies down upon its left side, and sleeps so whenever sleep overtakes and constrains it. But after the spring equinox it rests in the reverse position and lies upon its right side. So at each equinox the Ram changes its way of lying down.

The Phagrus and the Maeotes

The inhabitants of Syene regard the Phagrus as sacred, and those who dwell in Elephantine, as it is called, the Maeotes. (This also is a species of fish.) And the reverence which both peoples pay to either kind has its origin in this: when the Nile is about to rise and overflow.

These fish come swimming in advance, as though heralding the coming water, and gladden the anxious hearts of the Egyptians with fair hopes, being the first to realise the advent of the flood and foretelling it by some marvellous natural faculty.

Moreover the aforesaid peoples are accustomed to add, concerning their respect for the fish, that they never eat one another.

A Red Sea Shellfish

It seems that there are other Shellfish besides in the Red Sea, whose shells are not smooth but have certain grooves and hollows in them. These shells have sharp lips, and when they close they fit into one another, as they make the points interlock, so that it seems as if the teeth of two saws came together.

And so if they catch any fisherman swimming and bite any part of him they cut it off, even though there be a bone within the bitten part; more than that, if they bite at a joint, they cut it off at once; nor is that to be wondered at, for their bite is exceedingly sharp.

21. The Crocodile at Ombos and Apollinopolis

In Egypt there are some, like the people of Ombos, who venerate Crocodiles, and just as we regard the Olympian gods with awe, so do they these animals." And when, as often happens, their children are carried off by them, the people are overjoyed.

While the mothers of the unfortunates arc glad and go about in pride at having, I suppose, borne food and a meal for a god. But the people of Apollinopolis, a district of Tentyra, net the Crocodiles, hang them up on persea-trees (these are indigenous), flog them severely, mangling them with all the blows in the world, While the creatures whimper and shed tears; finally they cut them up and eat them.

The Crocodile, it seems, is pregnant for sixty days, and produces sixty eggs which it broods for as many days: it has that number of vertebrae in its spine, and they say that sixty sinews girdle its body, and it bears young ones the same number of times, and it lives for sixty years (I am reporting what the people of Egypt say and believe); one may reckon the teeth of this creature as sixty in number; during sixty days of every year it remains quiet in its lair and abstains from food.

The Crocodiles are accustomed to the people of Ombos, and those that are kept in the lakes made by the aforesaid people are obedient to their summons. And the people bring them the heads of the animals which they sacrifice-they themselves will never touch that part and throw them in, and the Crocodiles come leaping round them.

The inhabitants of Apollinopolis, on the contrary, detest the Crocodile, for they say that this was the shape assumed by Typho. Others however say that this is not the reason, but that a Crocodile carried off the daughter of King Psammyntus, a supremely good and righteous man, and, therefore in memory of that disaster even posterity abhors the whole race of Crocodiles.

22. The Vulture

The Vaccaei(they are a western people) insult the corpses of such as die from disease as having died a cowardly and effeminate death, and dispose of them by burning; whereas those who laid down their lives in War they regard as noble, heroic, and full of valour, and them they cast to the Vultures, believing this bird to be sacred.

And when Romulus on the Palatine Hill, divining by the flight of twelve Vultures, had received a favourable augury, following the number of the birds he decreed that the rulers of Rome should be preceded by a number of rods equal to that of the birds seen on that occasion.

And the Egyptians believe that the Vulture is sacred to Hera, and deck the head of Isis with Vultures' feathers, and on the roofs of the entrances to their temples they carve the wings of Vultures in relief. I have earlier on said much concerning this bird, but not to the same effect.

23. The Scorpions of Coptos

At Coptos in Egypt the natives pay homage to Isis in a variety of rituals but especially in the service and ministry rendered by women who are mourning either a husband or a son or a brother.

And at Coptos there are scorpions of immense size, possessing very sharp stings, and most dangerous in their attack (for when they strike they kill instantly), and the Egyptians contrive innumerable devices for self-protection.

But although the women in mourning at the temple of the goddess sleep on the floor, go about with bare feet, and all but tread on the aforesaid scorpions, yet they remain unharmed. And these same people of Coptos Worship and deify the female gazelle, though they sacrifice the male. They say that the females are the pets of Isis.

The Crocodile

The Crocodile (I may say that I have learned these facts in addition to what has already been recounted of this animal) is naturally timid, of an evil disposition, and thoroughly villainous.

It is alert to seize and plan against its victims, but it dreads all noises and is afraid even of loud shouts of men and has a violent fear of those who boldly attack it.

Killed at Tentyra

Now the people of Egypt called Tentyrites know the best way to master the beast: the most effective way of wounding it is to strike it in the eyes or the armpits and even in the belly. Its back however, and its tail are impenetrable, for it is, fortified and, so to say, armed with scaly plates which resemble hard earthenware or shells.

Now the aforesaid people are so assiduous in pursuit of these creatures that the river in their district is left in profound peace by the Crocodiles. So there they make bold to swim and sport in their swimming.

Worshipped at Coptos

Whereas among the people of Ombos or Coptos or Arsinoe it is not easy even to wash one's feet nor can one draw water in security; why, one cannot even walk along the river banks freely and off one's guard. But the people of Tentyra worship Hawks.

For that reason those who live in Coptos, wishing to annoy the Tentyrites as enemies of the Crocodiles, often crucify Hawks. The Crocodile the people of Coptos liken to water, that is why they worship it; whereas the Tentyrites liken the Hawk to fire, hence their adoration.

And they adduce as evidence . . . maintaining that fire and water cannot mingle. Such are the marvellous tales told by the Egyptians.

The Dog-faces

After traversing the Egyptian oasis one is confronted for seven whole days with utter desert. Beyond this lives the human Dog-faces b along the road that leads to Ethiopia. It seems that these creatures live by hunting gazelles and antelopes; further, they are black in appearance, and they have the head and teeth of a dog.

And since they resemble this animal, it is very natural that I should mention them here. They are however not endowed with speech, but utter a shrill squeal. Beneath their chin hangs down a beard; we may compare it with the beards of dragons, and strong and very sharp nails give an edge to their hands. Their whole body is covered with hair-another respect in which they resemble dogs. They are very swift of foot and know the regions that are inaccessible: that is why they appear so hard to capture.

24. The Wolf

The neck of a Wolf is short and compressed; the animal is thus incapable of turning but always looks straight ahead. And if it wants to look back at any time, it turns its whole body. It has the sharpest sight of any animal, and indeed it can even see at night when there is no moon.

Hence the name Lycophos (wolf's-light, i,e. gloaming) is applied to that season of the night in which the Wolf alone has - light with which Nature provides him. And I think that Homer gives the name 'twilight of the night,' to the time during which Wolves can see to move about.

Beloved of Apollo

And they say that the Wolf is beloved of the Sun; and there are those who assert that the Ammo year is called Lycabas in honour of this animal. It is said also that Apollo takes pleasure in the Wolf, and the reason which is commonly reported has reached me too.

It is this: they say that the god was born after Leto had changed herself into a she−wolf. That is why Homer speaks of 'the wolf−born lord of the bow' [IL 4. 101]. That is why, as I learn, at Delphi a bronze Wolf is set up, in allusion to the birth-pangs of Leto.

Reveals Sacrilege

Others however deny this, maintaining that it was because a Wolf gave information that offerings had been stolen from the temple and had been buried by the sacrilegious thieves.

For it made its way into the temple and with its mouth pulled one of the priests by his sacred robe and drew him to the spot in which the offerings had been hidden, and then proceeded to dig the spot with its forepaws.

Get All The Books In The Series:

Animal Peculiarity Volume1 Part [1-8]
Animal Peculiarity Volume2 Part [1-8]
Animal Peculiarity Volume 3 Part [1-8]